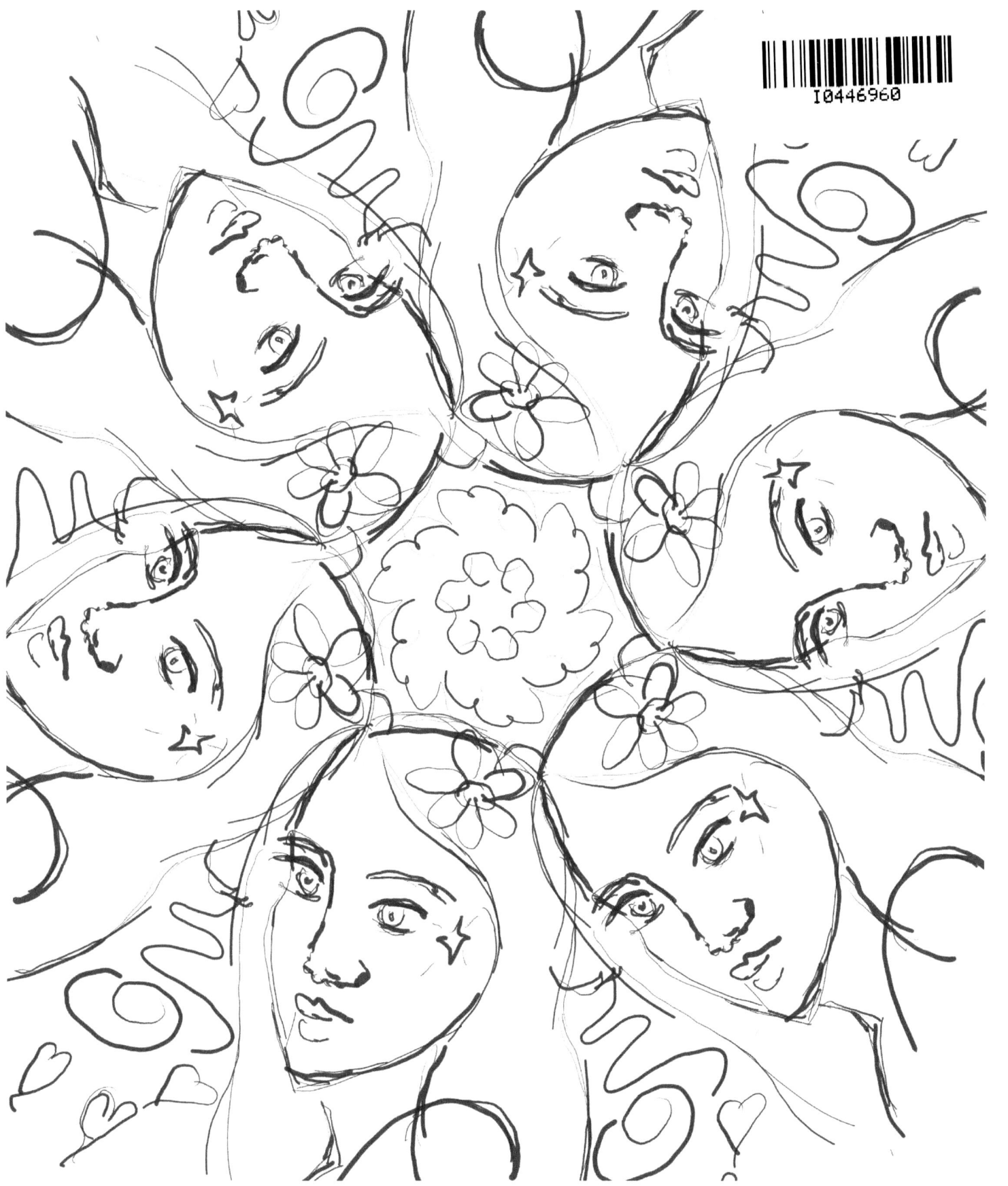

Perfection is overrated.

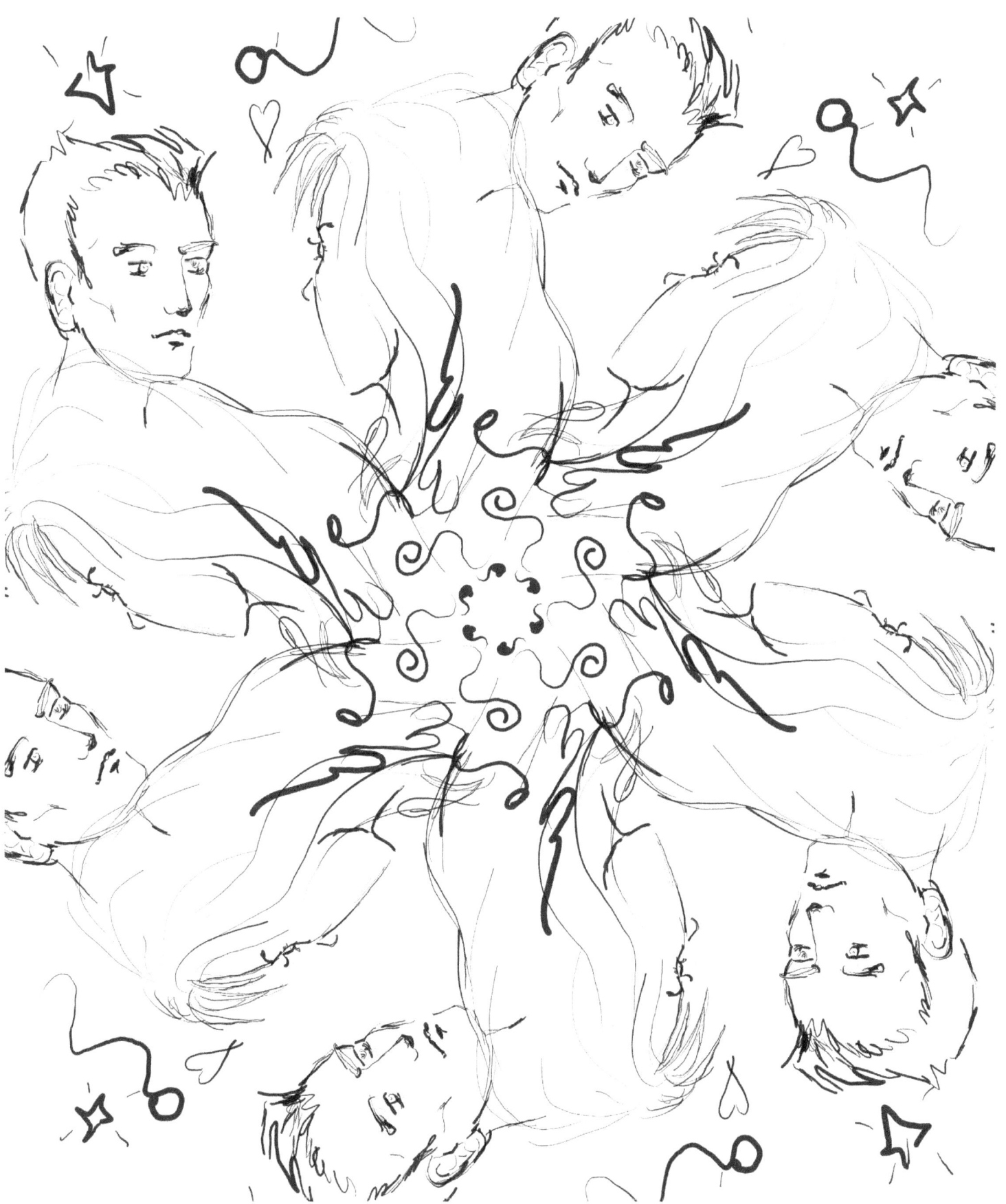

Don't always do your best. Save your best for the people who deserve it.

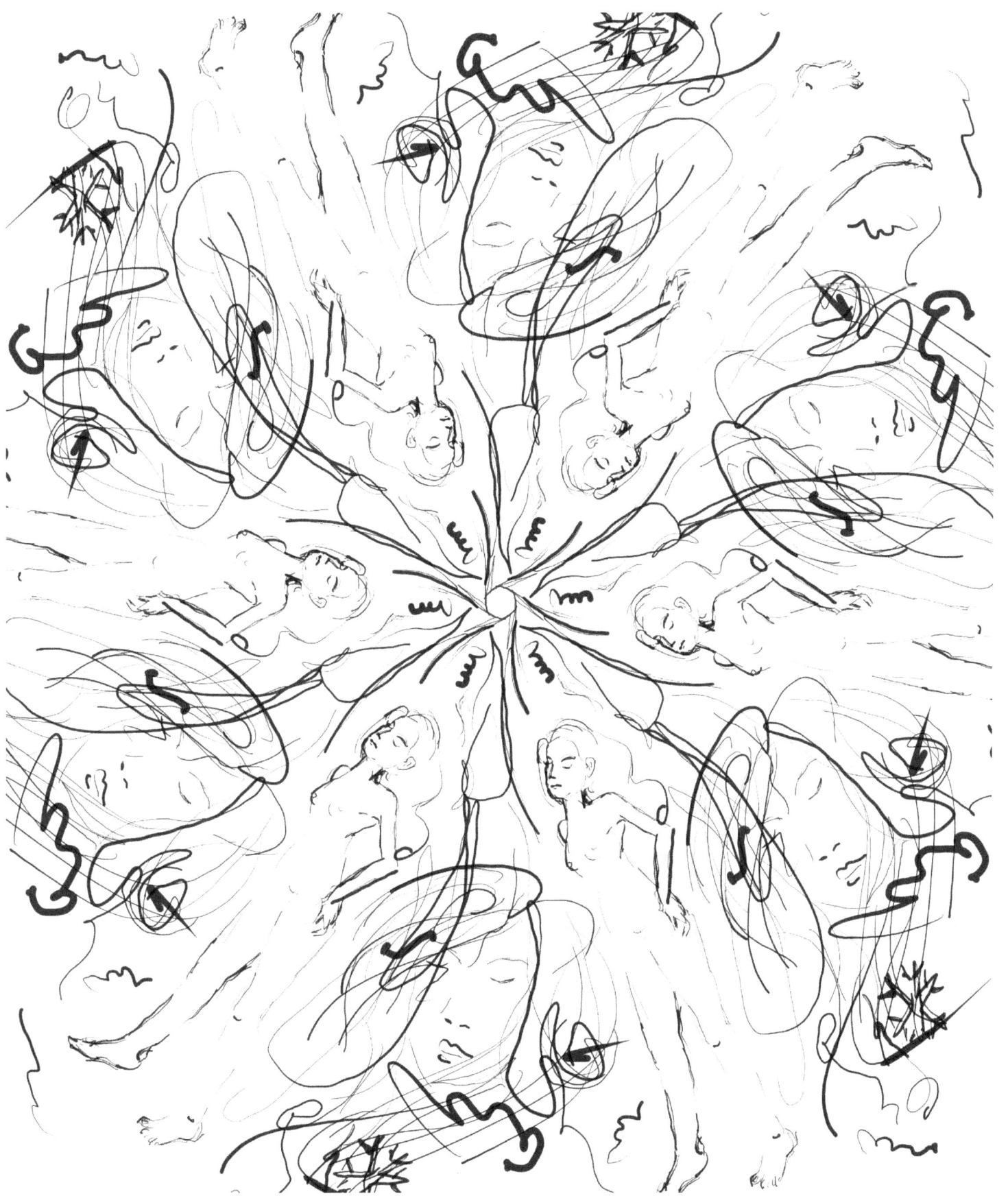

You don't have to be happy all the time.

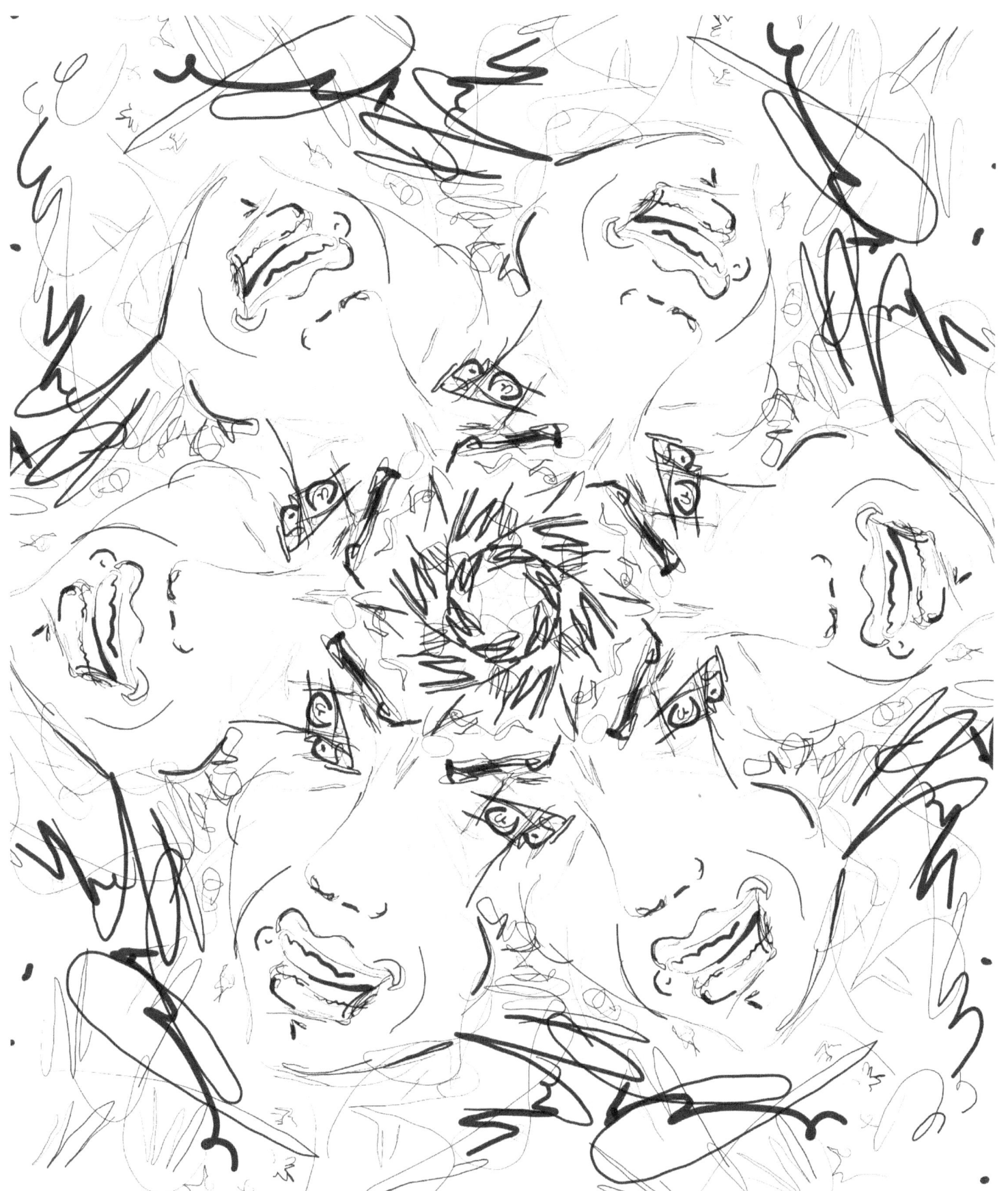

Feel all the feelings.

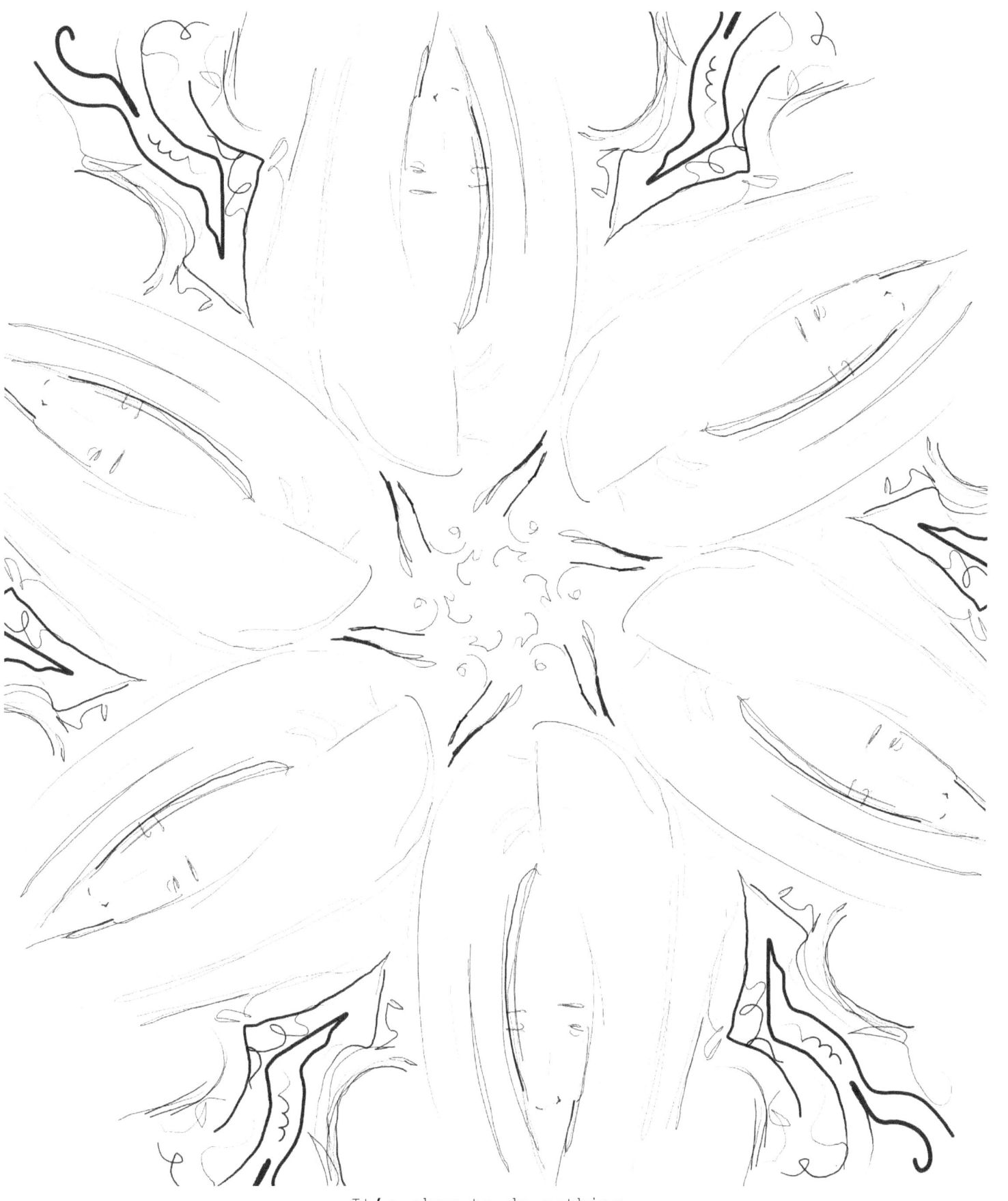

It's okay to do nothing.

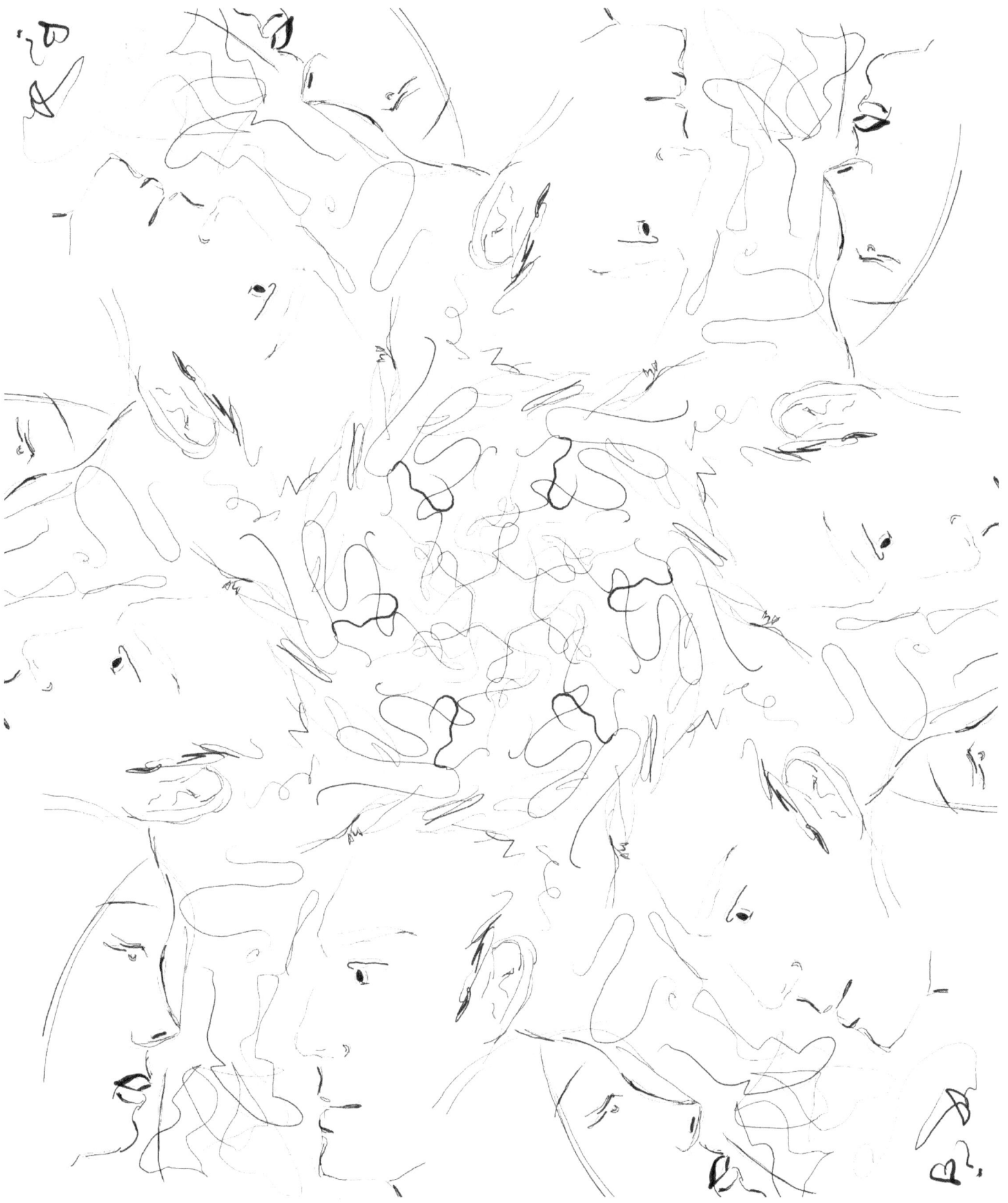

You don't have to be everything to everyone. You can be something to someone.

…Or nothing to no one…or nothing to everyone…or everything to no one…or everything to someone…or nothing to someone…or something to everyone…

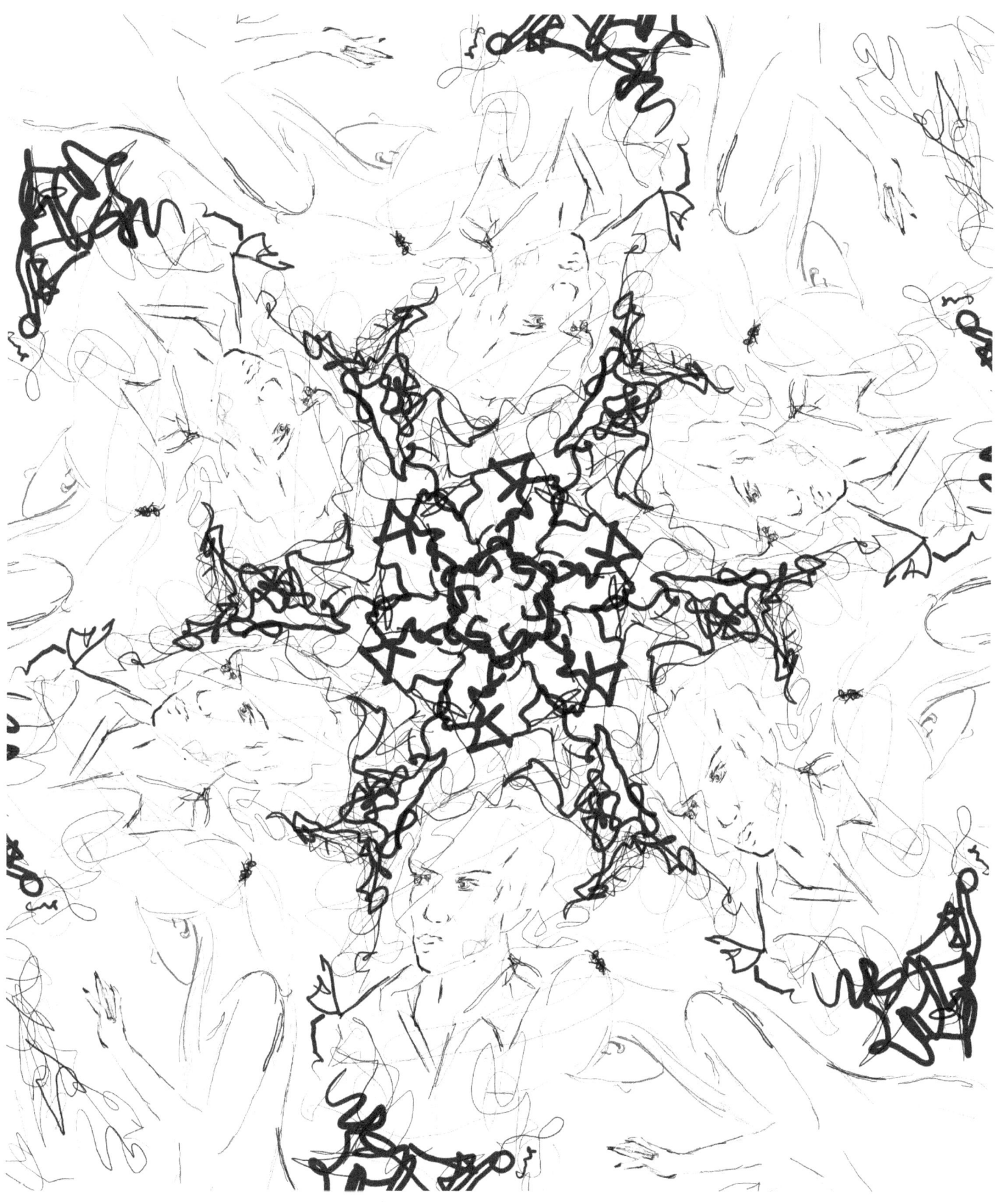

Do it because you want to.

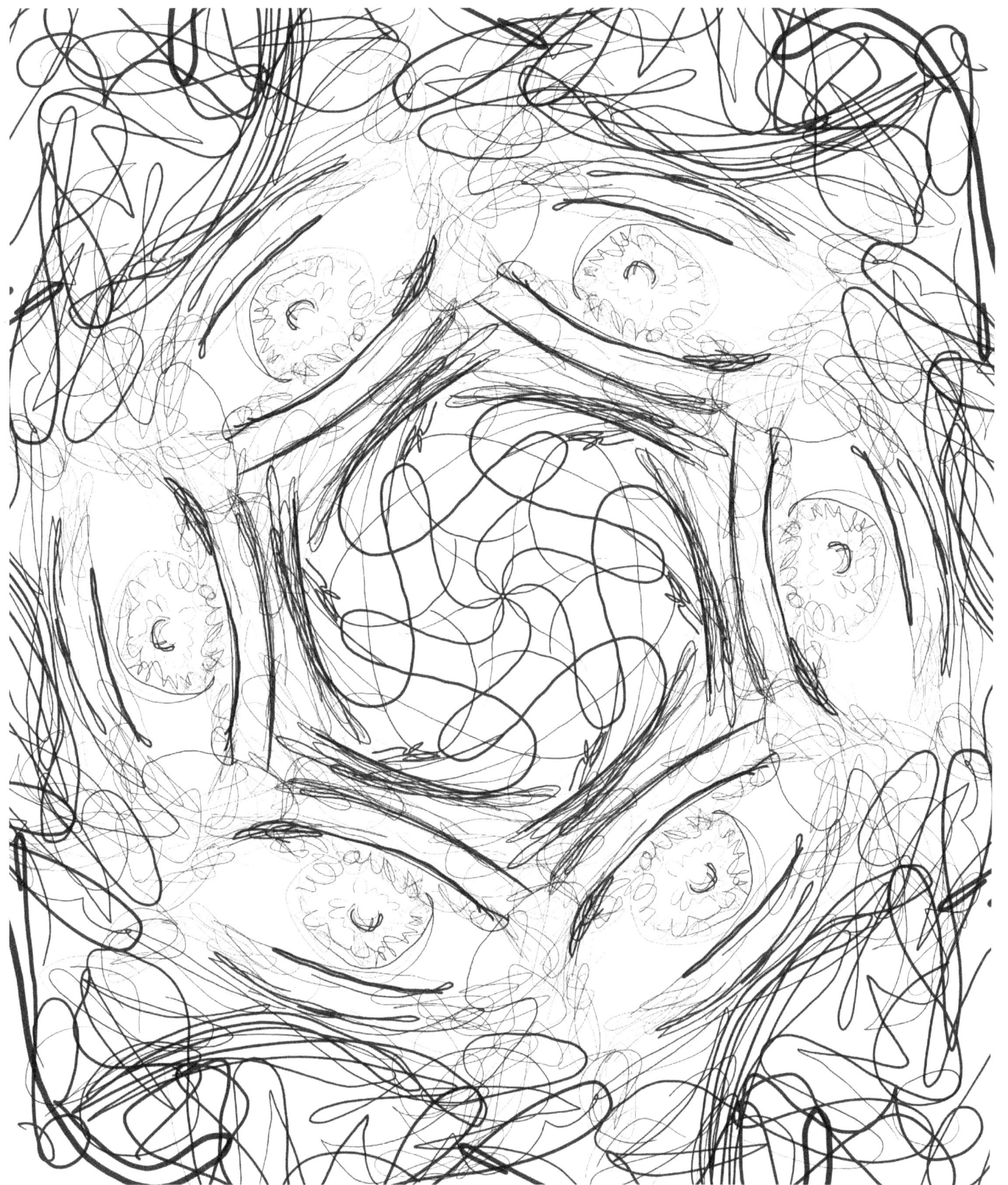

Everything you've ever seen, all of the colors, is a tiny slice of the electromagnetic spectrum.
Imagine if you could see everything.

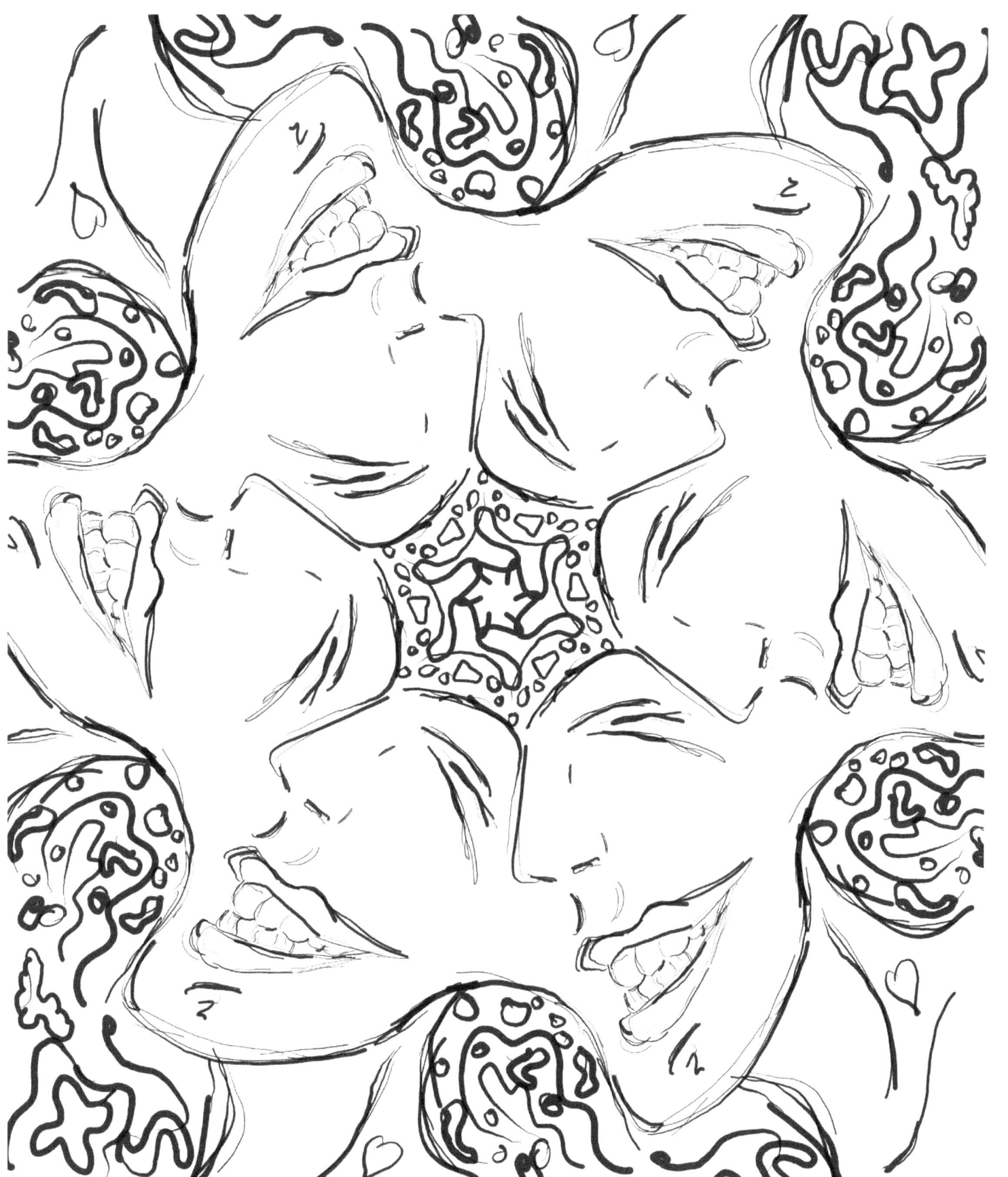

Feel everything.

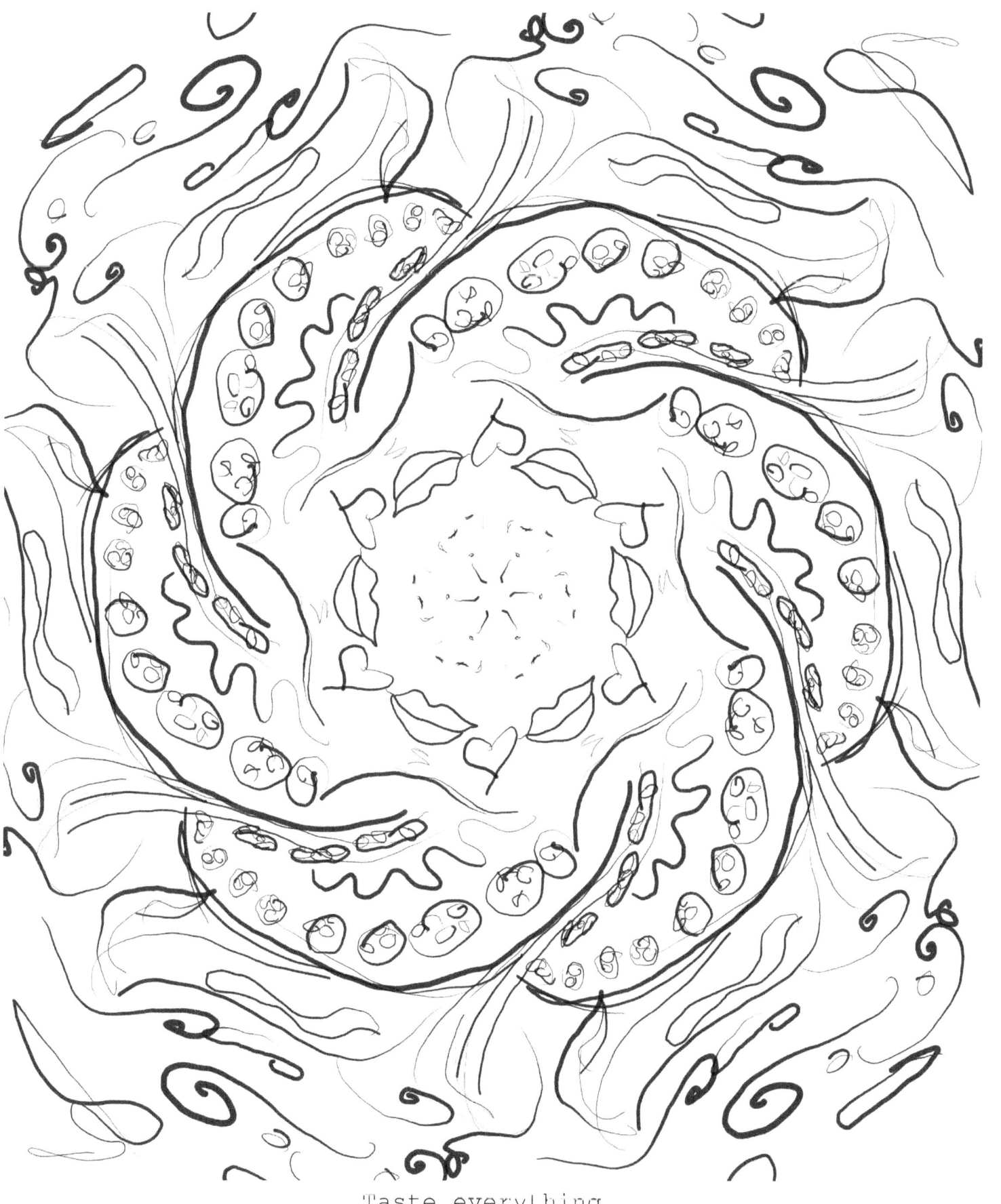

Taste everything.

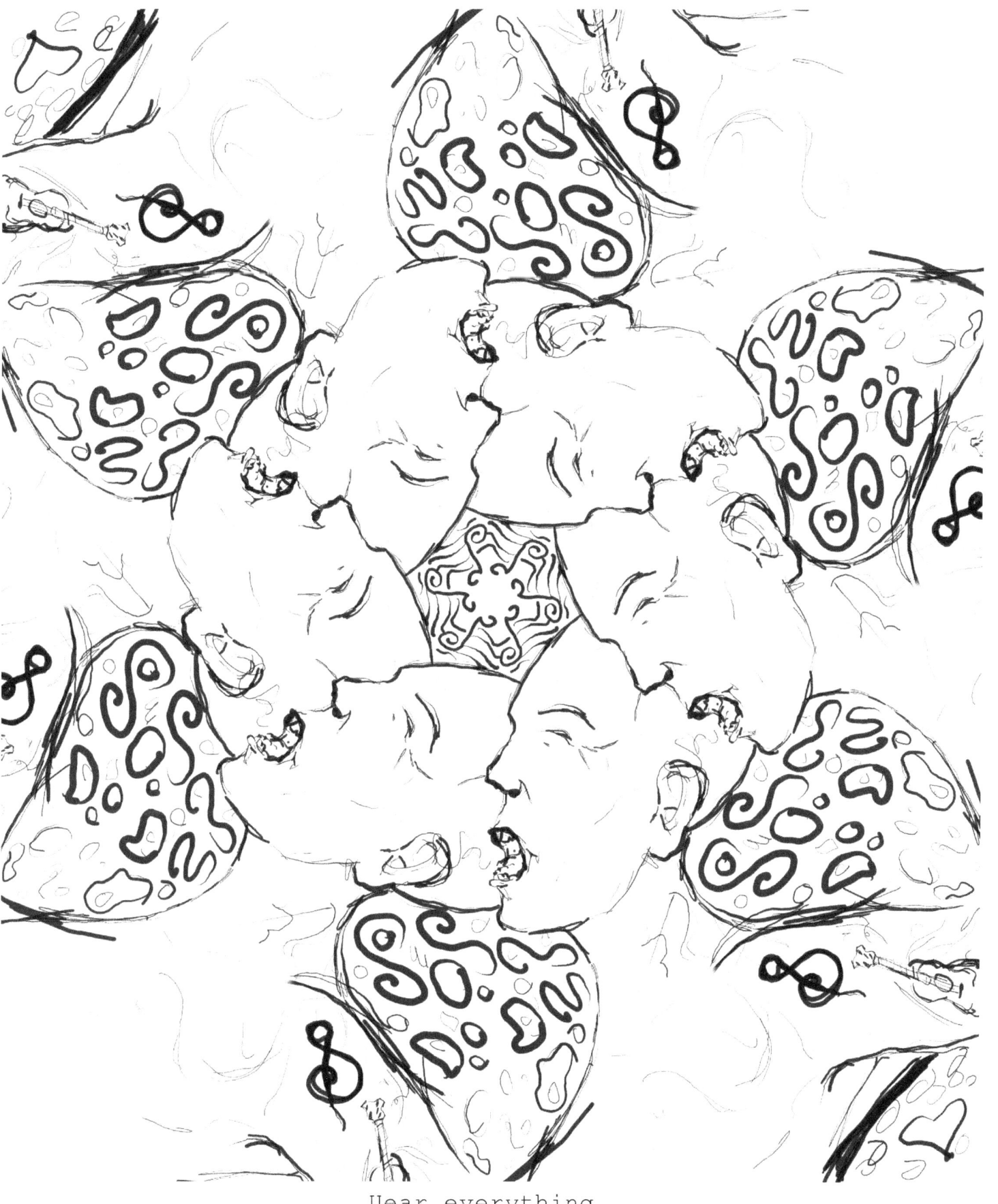

Hear everything.

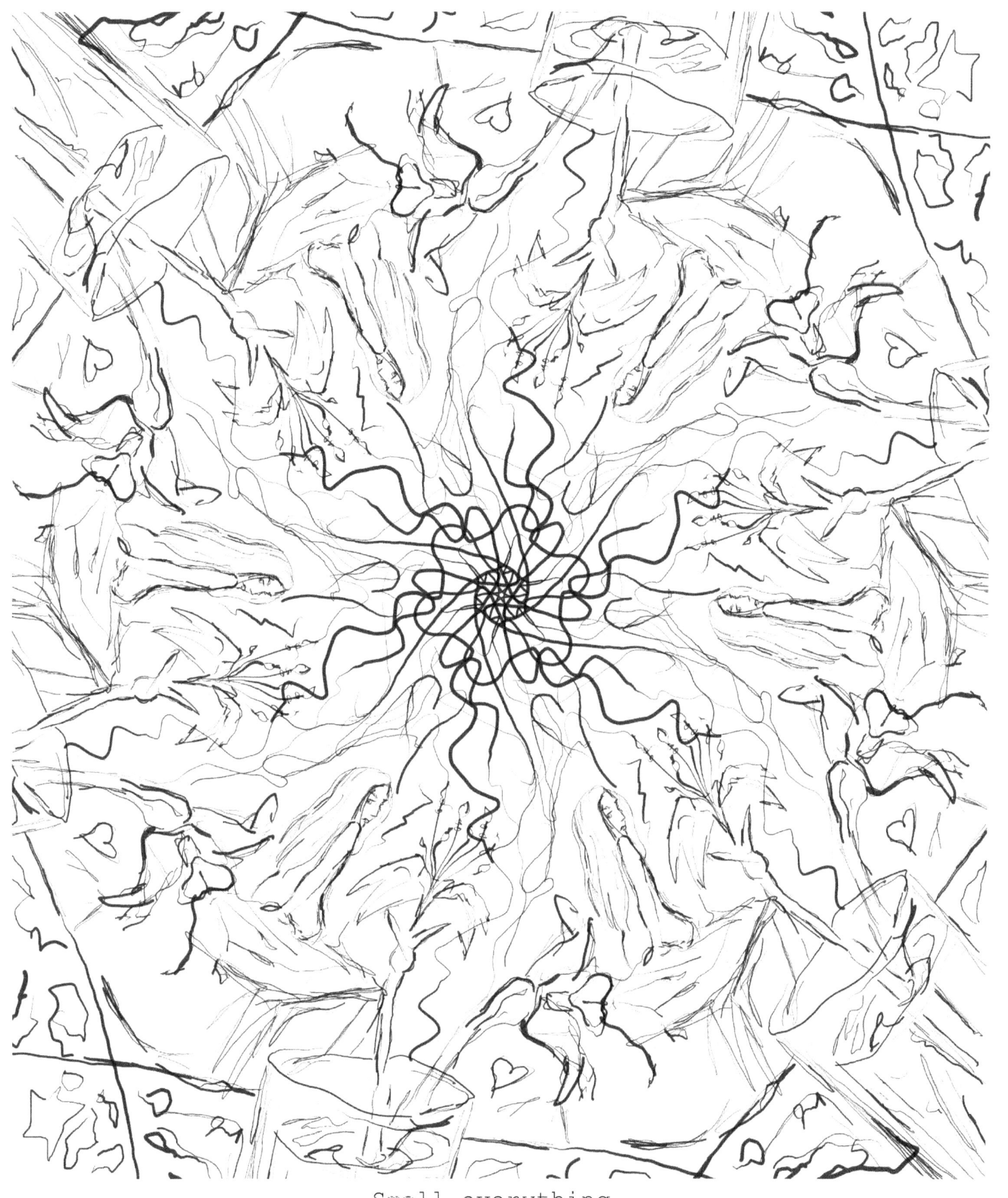

Smell everything.

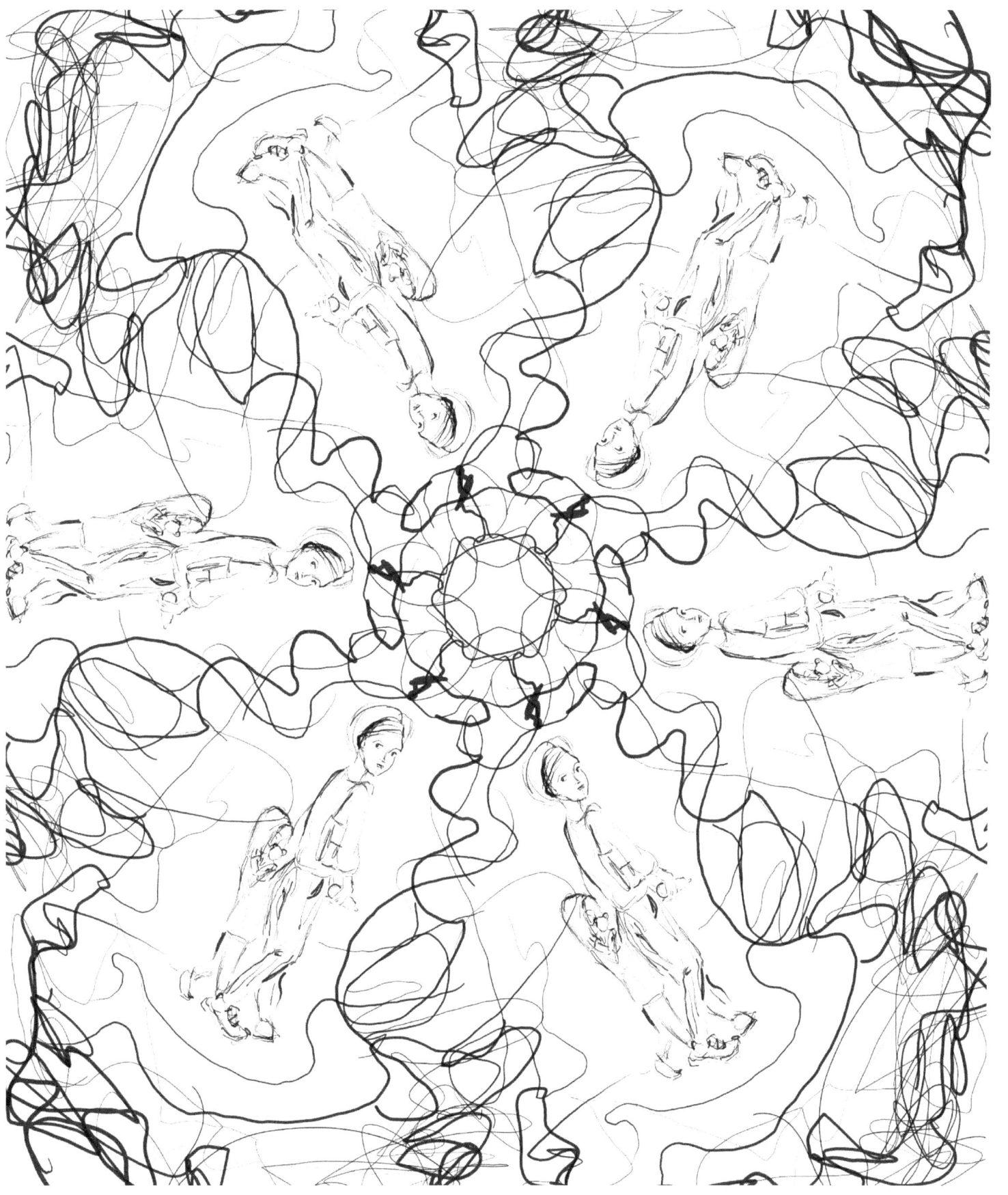

And then...nothing.

You do you.